Printed in Great Britain
by Amazon

33108402R00062